haiku Emily!

haiku Emily!

HAIKU-INSPIRED
POETRY BASED ON
THE WORK OF
EMILY DICKINSON

by Everett Decker

To Terry and Jasmine

Enjoy!

Everett Decker

Small Batch Books
Amherst, Massachusetts

Book design and cover image by Bhairavi Patel

Published December 10, 2011

ISBN 978-1-937650-05-6
Library of Congress Control Number 2011943772

SMALL
BATCH
BOOKS

493 SOUTH PLEASANT STREET
AMHERST, MASSACHUSETTS 01002
413.230.3943
SMALLBATCHBOOKS.COM

To Janet Larese,
my seventh-grade English teacher:
A nudge at just the right moment
can redirect your life.

CONTENTS

PREFACE

My captivation with Emily Dickinson began before I was even a teenager, about the same time I began writing poetry. Although I knew little of the "Belle of Amherst," growing up just twenty-five miles from where she had lived, I felt a kinship.

As I developed my own writing style, I experimented with many techniques. By the 1990s I was studying Japanese philosophy and naturally became interested in haiku. I quickly gravitated toward writing haiku-like poetry. In 2005, motivated by the book *The Haiku Year*, by Michael Stipe, et al., I dedicated myself to writing at least one haiku per day. Armed with a tiny notepad and a pen in my pocket, I composed 1,200 haiku that year.

More recently, I wanted to better acquaint myself with the life of Emily Dickinson and her poetry. One September I attended the annual Emily Dickinson Poetry Marathon, hosted by the Emily Dickinson Museum in Amherst, where participants read aloud each of the 1,789 known Dickinson poems. I participated in the final seven hours of the event (which went for seventeen hours that year) and was amazed at the breadth and scope of her work. I made a commitment that evening that I would read every poem by Emily Dickinson.

With R.W. Franklin's *The Poems of Emily Dickinson* in hand, I set out on my journey. It wasn't long before I realized I needed to regularly consult Noah Webster's 1844 *American Dictionary of the English Language* (the same edition used in the Dickinson household) just to tunnel into an Emily Dickinson poem. I also drew upon a comprehensive website run by linguist Cynthia Hallen, of Brigham Young University, called the Emily Dickinson Lexicon, which has a dictionary with more than 9,000 words as Emily Dickinson uniquely defined them in her poems. I soon found myself augmenting these resources with others and quickly built up a small library of Emily Dickinson reference material. As I labored through each poem, I would write definitions, historical information, and other pertinent notes in the margin of the book to better understand and to build some context around the poem. The purpose was to gain some insight into what her poem might be saying both literally and metaphorically.

As my enthusiasm toward Emily Dickinson's poetry grew and I attempted to share this with others, I discovered that without some of the resources I had depended on, the poems were a bit inaccessible to many. I found this frustrating due to my belief that Emily's poetry is still relevant and deserves more attention.

It was at about that time that I began to notice the similarities between haiku and Emily Dickinson's poetry. Both possess a deep connection to nature; both are untitled; and both are relatively short and dense (most of Dickinson's are approximately twelve lines, most haiku are three lines). Both styles are passive in that they simply present themselves and require that the reader approach the poem in order to get something out of it. This may be why Emily Dickinson is so popular in Japan.

I thought it would be fascinating to combine elements of haiku with elements of the hymnal lyric style used by Emily Dickinson. It was then that *haiku Emily!* was born. If I could distill a Dickinson poem into something less challenging, it might encourage the reader to approach her original poem.

Each *haiku Emily!* then, is based on a specific Emily Dickinson poem. While a *haiku Emily!* is neither haiku nor Emily Dickinson poetry, it is strongly influenced by both. Some lean more toward the unrhymed, less metrical, said-in-a-single-breath Eastern form; others lean more to the iambic feet and rhyme often used in mid-nineteenth century poetry. The *haiku* elements are: brief form (if a Dickinson poem used two or more images to support an idea, I chose the most prominent one); no title (already common to both); a connection to nature (inherent in both); use of everyday language (probably one of the most important aspects of a *hE!*); minimal use of capital letters or punctuation (perhaps the most noticeable difference between the two); and enough allure for the reader to want to engage with the poem (also common to both types). The *Emily!* elements are: direct evolution from a specific, identifiable Emily Dickinson poem (aligned with the Franklin numbering system); preservation of the central image (and refraining from adding anything not present in the original);

and retention of the use of rhyme and meter when appropriate.

The *haiku Emily!* poems usually took one of three directions: They either followed the original Emily Dickinson poem in design and content, albeit simplified (restate = 30 percent); they sustained the original intent but accomplished it in a different way, such as with an alternate format, a slightly narrowed concentration, etc. (refocus = 50 percent); much less frequently they used the essence of her poem and went in an entirely different direction (redirect = 20 percent).

I tried to adhere to several goals and criteria. Obviously, all could not be achieved in any single poem but, in general, I made an effort to keep the following things in mind: I sought to burrow down to what may have been the initial inspiration for the poem, holding onto the kernel while stripping away her craft (to reduce, then reconstitute), usually leaving out one jewel for the reader to discover in Emily's poem. If the poem wanted to have a more haiku-like expression, I tried to give it that. If the poem lent itself more to being *Emily!*, I strove to pay tribute to the rhythmic hymnal quality of the original along with a similar rhyming pattern (I rarely attempted to duplicate her slant rhyme, however). As it turned out, about 40 percent of the *hE!* poems are more haiku-like, another 40 percent are a single quatrain, and the remaining 20 percent are longer than four lines. Almost all are considerably shorter than the originals. I was mindful to utilize only language that would have been used in Emily's time (although I did depart on rare occasions). Likewise, only inventions of her era were used.

hE! is a means to lead the reader to Emily Dickinson, to see her genius, her craft, her significance, the extent and wealth of her poetry. I held no preconception about where a *haiku Emily!* was going to go or even how it would get there, but I trusted that each would speak to me and find its voice. I often tried to pick up on and pay homage to a particular component that Emily seemed to explore (meter, rhyme pattern, alliteration, etymology, structure, etc.). In the end, the hope was that a fresh poem would grow from where the Emily Dickinson one had been.

For some, Emily Dickinson is sacred, for others, she is intimidating. It is with the utmost respect and admiration for Emily's work that I have undertaken this project. My belief is that in order to offer her poetry to more readers, to make it more accessible, and to keep her poetry alive, I needed to approach (perhaps breach) that sacred ground. I may have had to make her less reverent to make her more relevant. For someone to linger long enough to appreciate the immensity and daring of her poetry, they first must pause. However short I may fall of this aspiration, if even a whisper of Emily that you might not otherwise have heard comes through, then I will feel that I have sung her praises as best I could. It matters less if you like *haiku Emily!* and more if there is a discussion surrounding the two poems and whether or not it ultimately directs you back to Emily Dickinson's poetry.

Another facet of the project is to bring Emily Dickinson's poetry into the classroom. The idea is for an ED/*hE!* pair to be introduced and a dialogue to be generated around them. (What are the likenesses and differences? What decisions were made in constructing the *haiku Emily!* and why? Does the *hE!* improve your comprehension of the Dickinson poem?) Almost accidently, students will need to delve into the Emily Dickinson poem and learn more about poetry, and certainly Dickinson's poetry, in the process. The final step in that progression would be for the students then to create their own poems in response to the pairs, and in so doing acquire even more understanding of the structure and elements of poetry.

Personally, this journey has brought me closer to Emily Dickinson's poetry than I had ever imagined. When I was twelve, I bicycled to Amherst looking for Emily. I find myself still searching, yet with an ever-increasing fascination of her and an admiration for her poetry that deepens the further I dig. Somewhere early along that exploration, she rekindled my love of language.

—*Everett Decker*

ACKNOWLEDGMENTS

First and foremost, I would like to acknowledge my indebtedness to Emily Dickinson. There never would have been a *haiku Emily!* without her poetry.

If Lavinia, Emily's sister, had not recognized the value of the cache of poetry discovered after the poet's death and labored to get them published, her work likely would never have surfaced.

Likewise, if Mabel Loomis Todd and Thomas Wentworth Higginson had not "regularized" Emily's poems in the first publications, she may have been marginalized as a poet, the public not being ready to accept or appreciate her innovations at the time.

The herculean task taken on by Thomas H. Johnson in the mid 1950s, to collect all known existent Dickinson poems in one volume in their original form, assured a place for Emily Dickinson as one of the greatest poets of all time.

R.W. Franklin, likewise, in the late 1990s, updated Johnson's work with an additional fourteen poems and with more accurate dating. Franklin's editions are becoming the new standards for Dickinson readers and scholars alike. It is his *Reading Edition* that my collection is based on.

Cynthia Hallen's work in creating the Emily Dickinson Lexicon website (edl.byu.edu) has been indispensible as a resource. Having the lexicon as well as Webster's 1844 *American Dictionary of the English Language* available has been essential to my burrowing through Emily's poems.

Cindy Dickinson, the director of interpretation and programming at the Emily Dickinson Museum, and Jane Wald, the executive director of the museum (emilydickinsonmuseum.org), have both been supportive of my efforts from the beginning. Their work in preserving the legacy of Emily Dickinson and spreading her reach are tireless.

From its inception, Missy-Marie Montgomery, Ph.D., got what *haiku Emily!* was about. Her personal and professional support played a large part in keeping me enthused throughout the arduous process of creating the

1,789 *hE!*. Missy then dedicated countless hours poring over hundreds of *haiku Emily!* and their associated Emily Dickinson poems in order to help me narrow the choices down for this first publication, and to give critical analysis of the selections.

In the crucial last stages of this project, Anne Melanson threw herself into the fray and lent her critical skills in helping to select and edit the final *hE!*

I would be remiss if I didn't also mention Midori Asahina, Polly Longsworth, and Susan Snively, each Dickinson scholars who gave me valuable feedback on the project.

Finally, I want to thank Trisha Thompson and Fred Levine at Small Batch Books. Their expertise in the publishing end has been an important aspect of the finished product.

haiku Emily!

h&!

0004

this spring a robin in my tree
but by the summer gone
to master through the year a song
'fore it returns to me

J5/FR4 *I have a bird in spring*

0005

I have a sister true as blood
who lives a house away
and like a wondrous flower bud
she blossoms every day

 J14/FR5 *One sister have I in the house*

2

hey!

0010

the laurel's for distinguished few
and garland's for the Queen
the rest will have to just make do
with roses shared between

J34/FR10 *Garlands for queens may be*

0018

I draw the curtains
a ruffle of feathers
Blast

J27/FR18 *Morns like these we parted*

hει!

0021

my parting
unlike the maple's
is silent

J18*/FR21 *The gentian weaves her fringes*
(*Johnson 18 = Franklin 21, 22, 23)

0039

twice I have been bankrupt Lord
and stood before your door
I can scarcely now afford
to beg of you once more

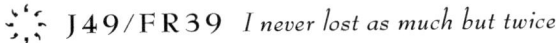 J49/FR39 *I never lost as much but twice*

6

0041

this quiet village all of stone
stiller now that I am here
cooler than my former home
but just a throw from there

J51/FR41 *I often passed the village*

hc!
0049

Katie walks with six legs
and ne'er an empty knee
when Katie asks the Lord to bless
it's not for one but three

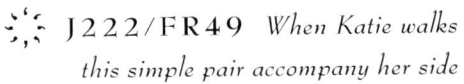 J222/FR49 *When Katie walks*
this simple pair accompany her side

h&*!*
0064

Heart, let's both forget him
you his warmth and I his light
but please make haste for if you lag
I'll remember him tonight

J47/FR64 *Heart we will forget him*

9

*h& /
& !*

0074

my bouquet I will not send
until my hands are silent
flowers open as they tend
mine, just not before I meant

J95/FR74 *My nosegays are for captives*

10

0084

a small child
a small box
a big hole

J146/FR84 *On such a night or such a night*

0086

the wren must have the finest nest
the lark a modest home is best
and though the latter makes less lofty choices
every morning she rejoices

J143/FR86 *For every bird a nest*

hE!

0113

I love the butterflies and bees
the brooks, the breeze
the breath of trees

why this rainy day if they love me?

J111/FR113 *The bee is not afraid of me*

0127

past my flower garden
the local children prance
after, when they're in their beds
the flowers' turn to dance

J133/FR127   *As children bid the guest good night*

14

he!

0133

quiet the coronation
silent I did sing
to my own fascination
slowly – you my king

⁎ J151/FR133 *Mute thy coronation*

0135

I am not a fool for fame
just a little for the soul
the tiny bit of bread I claim
more filling than the whole

J159/FR135   *A little bread a crust a crumb*

0160

not for praying
we both hang our heads
but for lying

J105/FR160 *To hang our head ostensibly*

0163

if by love, I heaven keep
why, then, work or sleep?
if to dream of you is blessed
why, then, do the rest?

✦ J109/FR163 *By a flower by a letter*

18

0182

the sun
so moving
     it set

J152/FR182 *The sun kept stooping stooping low*

0193

ears deceived by what they hear
eyes by what they see
the heart with all that extra weight
not moved so easily

J688/FR193 *Speech is a prank of parliament*

0225

I went from girl to be a "wife"
and auctioned off that other life
this now is heaven, so I'm told
and no reclaiming what was sold

J199/FR225 *I'm wife I've finished that*

hE!

0244

yes, bee and I, we drink
more often than you'd think
we're not all ail and whine

sometimes a bitter
will make us feel better
and everything is fine

thirsty? don't you fear it
there's cheer for our spirits
and fruit still on the vine

so if we weave through the air
please don't despair
straight just isn't our kind of line

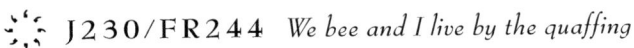 J230/FR244 *We bee and I live by the quaffing*

hey
0246

the sun caressed the morning
for hours she seemed to glow
a crown she wore upon her head
so everyone would know

when next she checked her headdress
the day was winding down
her king now bowed beside another
and she – no king, no crown

J232/FR246 *The sun just touched the morning*

0252

won't you consider a sparrow
that fitful, edged your way
not quite a friend, nor quite a foe
then death got in the way

my lips might stumble on the prayer
they fumble but aren't dumb
I might not be the first one there
but as earnest as they come

J237/FR252 *I think just how my shape will rise*

hey
0255

a drop of water in the sea
can lose its own identity
if I stay small, I think you'll see
that all, is all I need to be

J284/FR255 *The drop that wrestles in the sea*

0266

my coin and cloth, beloved books
I'd give it all for just one look
I'd give my Robin, Wren and Rose
I'd give you all of those

Daffodil, Daisy, Lark and Lily
the Mum, Marigold and Morning Glory
the Starling, Sparrow and the Crow
I'd let all of them go

all the months and even June
my bluest, highest noon
my Bee and Butterfly and Buttercup
I'd give all of that up

terra firm and firmament
my life and all it meant
to look an hour upon your face
my Kingdom for your sparing grace

J247/FR266 *What would I give to see his face*

hej

0271

strawberries!
over the fence

I could climb, but can't
he can't climb, but could
were I a boy — I would

I can't, for the dress
he just can't, I guess
even with the pants

over the fence
strawberries!

J251/FR271 *Over the fence*

0280

the narrow path
to God's altar
has such
a tight
corset

J493/FR280 *The world stands solemner to me*

hє!
0282

to know pine
is to know something
of oak

J320/FR282 *We play at paste*

0283

I should have had
a win without a loss
Heaven more than Earth
dove more than albatross
I should have had — would have liked
Christ without the cross

J313/FR283 *I should have been too glad I see*

hej

0292

I got so I could hear his name and not arrest
I could go where we had been and not protest
could move the letters and not be distressed
could do all that, I can attest

God, if there, may have shown his grace
answered a prayer I never placed
took care of my small misery
repaired that broken heart in me

J293/FR292 *I got so I could take his name*

hE!
0294

our break
from the hair shirt –
a bed of nails

∴ J264/FR294 *A weight with needles on the pounds*

h&!
0299

okay
there was the whole Eden thing –
get over it

J267/FR299   *Did we disobey him*

0310

paradise for me
behind the farthest hill
when I think I'm nearly there
I find it farther still

J239/FR310 *Heaven is what I cannot reach*

34

0330

after the wedding
everything was bridle

 J273/FR330   *He put the belt around my life*

35

0331

a ghost faintly seen
more a curtain than a shade
more sheer than sheen
a shadow not quite seen

a spirit in-between
something quick that fades
a wisp, a whisper made obscene
that left me quite afraid

J274/FR331 *The only ghost I ever saw*

0335

a smile
BURSTS –
but mine...

J514/FR335   *Her smile was shaped like other smiles*

0351

Bliss – the fat robin
   the slinky cat
            missed

 J507/FR351   *She sights a bird she chuckles*

0368

why the Sea
the Wagon Wheels
the distant Hills
and not me?

why the Fly
the Bees
the Trees
and not I?

why the Day
the Blossom
the bright Bells
and HE so far away?

why this crime
that you are kissed
that you are blessed
and He is yours, not mine!

J498/FR368   *I envy seas whereon he rides*

0370

in my garden there's a bird
that ne'er alights a rose
it suddenly appears, it jags
and then like that – it's froze

in front of its flower parked
its body still, its wings a whir
it drinks of its ambrosia
then darts off in a blur

did my dog and I imagine
such a fantastic sight?
he nears the still unsteady rose
revealing we were right!

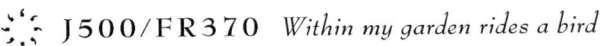 J500/FR370 *Within my garden rides a bird*

0373

there is something beyond our grasp
intangible as thought
as curious as a question
whose answer we cannot

and anyone who gets there
if anywhere there is
is just as stumped as we are
about the "there" this is

J501/FR373 *This world is not conclusion*

hE!
0377

Jesus, I have looked for you
quite nearly everywhere
why this game of hide and seek
if I don't have a prayer

J502/FR377   *At least to pray is left is left*

0387

the moon leads
her obedient sea
by gradual degrees

☼ J429/FR387   *The moon is distant from the sea*

43

0389

amazed, the day at Heaven's Gate
it opened as I came
my holiday, an annotate
my paradise, the fame
of welcome by forgetful saints
that yet recalled my name

0444

I am like a fly
except a bit more shy
and he eats more than I
and, of course, I don't fly
other than that
we're pretty much alike

J612/FR444 *It would have starved a gnat*

0445

Prose—
the cage
I fly out of!

J613/FR445 *They shut me up in prose*

0462

our spirit –
a bird that dances
in its flight

J653/FR462   *Of being is a bird*

hE!
0469

my garth of green
terrestrial sea
my emerald pearls –
sweet garden peas!

J484/FR469 *My garden like the beach*

48

h&!

0492

lend a hand to those who've fallen
hold the hand of those crestfallen
shake the hand of all who then
take your hand when you are them

J767/FR492   *To offer brave assistance*

49

hey!
0503

if I say that I misplaced you
and just, I need to find
then you, I'm only missing
instead, that you have died

J996/FR503 *We'll pass without the parting*

50

0505

they have a heartbeat
to me is rhythm — no is poetry
strongest just before you fall
into the space they leave

0530

a flower expects to die
will give its life to magnify
it's we who wonder, wince and weep
when the blossom doesn't keep
we who oft will quick omit
a life's sole prerequisite

 J567/FR530 *He gave away his life*

52

0533

first poets
then the sun
then – summer
and with heaven
the catalog is done

if I needed a shorter list
I'd end with number one

J569/FR533   *I reckon when I count at all*

0550

can theirs be a grief
as great as mine
does it weigh as much
or plague as wide a time

what is the source
of their affliction
and how grand
their crucifixion

does the torture turn to agony
then to misery then to suffering
before the hurt has mastery

or does the ache turn into pain
then anguish, then despair
before devastation reigns

how every dreadful breath we wrench
between the heartbreak of life
and the wretchedness of death

I don't know if your torment is as mine
but if the tailor is the same
it could have close design

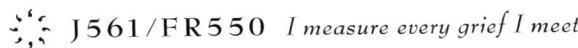 J561/FR550 *I measure every grief I meet*

54

hεɟ
0566

not her makeup
that makes her beautiful
but her makeup

J558/FR566   *But little carmine hath her face*

0591

there was a stillness when I died
except the buzz that was
eyes were dry
had wrung – were done
holding breaths to hear when death
consume the room
all the stage and just the fly
and I
he buzzed uncertain
I drew the curtain

J465/FR591   *I heard a fly buzz when I died*

56

0604

you'll know her – by her sketchy feet
you'll know her – by her vest
you'll know her – by the song so sweet
within the robin's breast

J634/FR604   *You'll know her by her foot*

h&!
0609

Night—
the long stretches between
when it's not

J471/FR609 *A night there lay the days between*

58

0653

imagine Resurrection Day
all those people
and only two lines!

J515/FR653 *No crowd that has occurred*

he!

0658

don't shun them Lord
who once spurned me
I forgive their ignorance
forgive them equally

J538/FR658   *Tis true they shut me in the cold*

h&!

0659

if you know despair's depth
you won't mistake defeat for death
if you came from the grave
you're qualified to save
if you have nothing you can teach
what right have you to preach

J539/FR659 *The province of the saved*

0664

Misery—
a wound
we love to pick at

0704

what I eat today is Defeat
a stew of blood and bone
replete with shell-shocked boys
and bruise and wound and stone

not like on the other side
strewn with Victory and Praise
those boys have more pride
and brighter trumpets at their graves

J639/FR704 *My portion is defeat today*

63

0779

give the flower by my side
all the beauty I might hide
let it blossom in my place
I will flourish from its grace

J707/FR779 *The grace myself might not obtain*

0785

not so much, I dropped it
or that the ground too hard
but that the plate not suited
held in such high regard

J747/FR785   *It dropped so low in my regard*

0839

the sun we trust
when not in sight
is right behind

why our faith
so hard to find?

J972/FR839 *Unfulfilled to observation*

0852

a grave unmarked, neglected
will have to wait for when
Resurrection's turning
tends that plot again

J876/FR852 *It was a grave yet bore no stone*

0902

our consciousness must travel
beyond our picket fence
for human hearts to see more
than white in deference

J911/FR902   *Too little way the house must lie*

hey!

0903

doubt is the darkness along a path
dreams let us see past that

 J859/FR903   *A doubt if it be us*

0919

if I die in spring—
it is enough

J845/FR919 *Be mine the doom*

0924

too soon for you to hurt
or really to understand
my fingers cold with dirt
trying to warm your tiny hand

J940/FR924 *On that dear frame the years had worn*

hE!
0926

from birth we have that wobbly walk
our experience seems to teach
an eye to keep from tumbling down
the other toward where we reach

J875/FR926   *I stepped from plank to plank*

hɛ!
0941

pond lilies
cradle
the still child

J923/FR941   *How the waters closed above him*

0965

how far it is
to heaven or hell
depends
on where you start

J929/FR965 *How far is it to heaven*

h&!
0975

oh, my morning rose
what happened to your shoot
'fore I could feast upon your blossom
a worm ate of your root

 J913/FR975 *And this of all my hopes*

0976

may it be the fairest month
that ever may have been
right after every April
may it come again

J977/FR976 *Besides this may*

h&!

0979

the humble Bumble off to work
to draw from waiting clover
he'll hum a tune along his cirque
until his day is over

J916/FR979   *His feet are shod with gauze*

0988

Death cared about the west the least
Passion had its own request
he liked to chase the sun, but couldn't in the east

since Death preferred the east the best
right there the discussion ceased
Death got all the east, and Passion got the rest

J1033/FR988 *Said death to passion*

0990

percussionists
will work for food
C.N.E. Woodpecker

☼ J1034/FR990 *His bill an augur is*

1033

a rigorous climb
aided only
by the view

h&!

1040

one glory—
I was yours

J1028/FR1040   *Twas my one glory*

1054

do you prefer a velvet cheek
or one of ivory
or might you fancy a freckled one
like the one on me

 J1094/FR1054 *Themself are all I have*

1109

the sun set — no witness but I
the sun rose — I and a bird
counting her majesty — a third

J 1079 / F R 1109 *The sun went down no man looked on*

1117

too tired to wander or to speak
your quiet arms so close, oh Death
no need for me to reach

J 1065/FR 1117 *Let down the bars oh death*

84

hey!

11 23

your life is more than but a form
like liquor in a mug
'tis better on the lips
than when it's in the jug

☼ J 1101/FR 11 23   *Between the form of life and life*

1172

in love –
it is the seconds
that make the our

☼ J 1248 / F R 11 7 2 *The incidents of love*

1174

a spider took up my residence
and made itself at home
and now I felt the visitor
and down the street did roam

to see if I could find a court
to hear me plead my case
that a spider had evicted me
from my living space

J1167/FR1174   *Alone and in a circumstance*

1197

Heroes—
those who when asked to rise
don't duck their head for fear of majesty

1218

if you lack conviction
for that you can't atone
better to be born again
with marrow in the bone!

J1274/FR1218   *The bone that has no marrow*

1220

a moment — no tomorrow
and neither has a past
the consequence another matter—
it can last and last

hey!

1233

the sadness that I carried
was much larger than I thought
were I to try to lift again
I think that I could not

J1197/FR1233   *I should not dare to be so sad*

hey!
1234

my memory has its windows
and plenty of rooms with doors
it doesn't mean I'll let you in
that's what locks are for

J1182/FR1234 *Remembrance has a rear and front*

hE!

1247

the almost is more thrilling
the close discover as you hide
the tingling breeze that runs your neck
as they very nearly find

J1175/FR1247 *We like a hairbreadth 'scape*

1284

hope
the long walk toward happiness
disappointment
a pebble in the shoe

J1264/FR1284   *This is the place they hoped before*

1286

no more frugal or fantastic
a traveler
than the book

⁖ J1263/FR1286 *There is no frigate like a book*

hey!
1297

a clover caught at first a bee
from sinking through the sky
a puff of wind
and with as much indifference
a clover and no bee

J1343/FR1297 *A single clover plank*

1300

Silence—
what's left
when we stop interrupting

J1251/FR1300 *Silence is all we dread*

1307

easy the ache
in hands of mine
an awkward grace
with near the rhyme

☼ J1313/FR1307 *Warm in her hand these accents lie*

98

1375

Enchantment—
nine parts longing
one delight

J1299/FR1375 *Delight's despair at setting*

1377

a rat haps
trap snaps
that's that

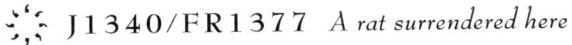 J1340/FR1377   *A rat surrendered here*

100

1402

the deepest hurt will see a dawn
the shallowest grave – none

 J1378/FR1402 *His heart was darker than the starless night*

1407

the tree his dining hall
the cutlery his teeth
we fancy we rise above the squirrel
though we stand far beneath

J1374/FR1407 *A saucer holds a cup*

h & !
1409

the faithful
sometimes a bit eager
for their martyrs

J1375/FR1409 *Death warrants are supposed to be*

1446

the ocean
never
sleeps
never
sleeps

J1428/FR1446 *Water makes many beds*

h&!
1460

a seed flies –
there will be a tomorrow

⁂ J1436/FR1460 *Than heaven more remote*

1469

the sun
respectfully rising –
rows of cold stones

J1443/FR1469   *A chilly peace infests the grass*

1478

a single note
struck well
beats the band

 NA/FR1478 *One note from one bird*

1484

before we even suspect it—singing
high in some bare tree
God – trumpeting in spring

J1465/FR1484 *Before you thought of spring*

1490

a feather at a time
the dandelion's down
resigns

 J1501/FR1490 *It's little ether hood*

1494

a secret
once uttered –
a regret

J1385/FR1494   *Secrets is a daily word*

1518

the ice storm
managing to freeze
all but the children

☼ J1498/FR1518 *Glass was the street in tinsel peril*

1545

it's the anticipation of spring
that has all the sting
the long song of silence
before the sing

J1530/FR1545 *A pang is more conspicuous in spring*

hey!
1575

now I lay here fast asleep
I pray the Lord it's not too deep
if I should die by a mistake
wake me up for heaven's sake!

✧ J1539/FR1575 *Now I lay thee down to sleep*

hε!
1591

if I should see a single bird
I am not alone
if I should hear it sing to me
all I need to own

NA/FR1591   *If I should see a single bird*

1613

meditation
fills the pond
we relax in

J1592/FR1613 *The lassitudes of contemplation*

1619

save the sober dresses
for when we die

⸭ J1572/FR1619 *We wear our sober dresses when we die*

1646

to compensate a life
Death will give to you despair
the only greater anguish
is when he buys a pair

✧ J1612/FR1646 *The auctioneer of parting*

1660

his voice still
his echo
still sounding

NA/FR1660   *But that defeated accent*

1676

a soul redressed
twice be blessed

hει!
1709

the trees I hadn't noticed
now hold the sun

☀ J1693/FR1709   *The sun retired to a cloud*

1724

so close he couldn't see his soul
so much farther was his mind
he resolved the matter with a hole
that left his corpse behind

J1686/FR1724 *The event was directly behind him*

1731

what form or presence do you take
what want or will hold dear
did you in your own image make
same hopes, same dreams, same fears

J1689/FR1731 *The look of thee what is it like*

1739

my whole life suddenly vacuous
a hawk tunnels toward its prey

J1655/FR1739 *Conferring with myself*

1758

love can raise the spirits
just not the dead

∴ J1731/FR1758 *Love can do all but raise the dead*

1769

she gave
a full stride
right to the grave

J1752/FR1769 *This docile one inter*

AFTERWORD

I completed the last *haiku Emily!* on 15 May 2011, the 125th anniversary of Emily Elizabeth Dickinson's death: it seemed only fitting that I should somehow commemorate that convergence. I cut some lilacs from my backyard, drove to the Homestead, and had the flowers placed in her room. After I obtained permission to cut some lilacs from her yard, I went to the West Cemetery and set those by her grave. I decided as a more lasting tribute, I would select 125 *haiku Emily!* for this first collection from the 1,789 poems created. Honoring her has been brought full circle by this book being published on the tenth of December, the anniversary of Emily Dickinson's birth.

For inclusion in this premier edition, a *haiku Emily!* had to pass my SIT test (i.e., can it *stand* on its own as a poem? Is it *interesting* either in its topic or in its presentation? And is it *tight*, condensed, and dense with image?). Additionally, I hoped to represent as wide a sampling of her subject matter as practical and span her entire canon. I also sought to include many *haiku Emily!* poems inspired by her lesser-known and seldom anthologized poetry.

My wish is that through *haiku Emily!* you become intrigued with Emily Dickinson. After you see her poetry from a new perspective, you may decide to reacquaint yourself with some of her poems and rediscover her genius as a poet. The journey can't help but be wonderful, if it ends up you have fun getting wherever it leads you—all the better!

—Everett Decker
Westfield, Massachusetts
30 October 2011

INDEX OF *haiku Emily!*
BY FIRST LINE

CROSS-REFERENCE
BY DICKINSON FIRST LINE

No Emily Dickinson poems appear in this publication. As an aid to locating the original Emily Dickinson poem that any particular *haiku Emily!* is based on (whether from the Johnson edition, the Franklin edition, or another source that uses the first line of her poem as the title), this cross-reference section has been provided. For the reader's convenience, associated cross-reference information has also been provided at the bottom of each page of *haiku Emily!* poems. There has been no attempt to reproduce any of the capitalization or punctuation as they might appear in the Emily Dickinson titles of the various sources.

Johnson #	Franklin #	Emily Dickinson title/first line	relates to *hE!* #
N/A	1676	A chastened grace is twice a grace	1676
1443	1469	A chilly peace infests the grass	1469
859	903	A doubt if it be us	0903
159	135	A little bread a crust a crumb	0135
471	609	A night there lay the days between	0609
1530	1545	A pang is more conspicuous in spring	1545
1340	1377	A rat surrendered here	1377
1374	1407	A saucer holds a cup	1407
1343	1297	A single clover plank	1297
264	294	A weight with needles on the pounds	0294
1167	1174	Alone and in a circumstance	1174
913	975	And this of all my hopes	0975
133	127	As children bid the guest good night	0127
502	377	At least to pray is left is left	0377
845	919	Be mine the doom	0919
1465	1484	Before you thought of spring	1484
977	976	Besides this may	0976
1101	1123	Between the form of life and life	1123
558	566	But little carmine hath her face	0566
N/A	1660	But that defeated accent	1660
109	163	By a flower by a letter	0163
1655	1739	Conferring with myself	1739
1375	1409	Death warrants are supposed to be	1409
1299	1375	Delight's despair at setting	1375
267	299	Did we disobey him	0299
143	86	For every bird a nest	0086
34	10	Garlands for queens may be	0010
1498	1518	Glass was the street in tinsel peril	1518

Johnson #	Franklin #	Emily Dickinson title/first line	relates to *hE!* #
567	530	He gave away his life	0530
273	330	He put the belt around my life	0330
47	64	Heart we will forget him	0064
239	310	Heaven is what I cannot reach	0310
514	335	Her smile was shaped like other smiles	0335
1034	990	His bill an augur is	0990
916	979	His feet are shod with gauze	0979
1378	1402	His heart was darker than the starless night	1402
929	965	How far is it to heaven	0965
923	941	How the waters closed above him	0941
498	368	I envy seas whereon he rides	0368
293	292	I got so I could take his name	0292
5	4	I have a bird in spring	0004
465	591	I heard a fly buzz when I died	0591
1022	1033	I knew that I had gained	1033
561	550	I measure every grief I meet	0550
49	39	I never lost as much but twice	0039
51	41	I often passed the village	0041
569	533	I reckon when I count at all	0533
313	283	I should have been too glad I see	0283
1197	1233	I should not dare to be so sad	1233
875	926	I stepped from plank to plank	0926
237	252	I think just how my shape will rise	0252
N/A	1591	If I should see a single bird	1591
199	225	I'm wife I've finished that	0225
747	785	It dropped so low in my regard	0785
876	852	It was a grave yet bore no stone	0852
612	444	It would have starved a gnat	0444
1501	1490	It's little ether hood	1490
1065	1117	Let down the bars oh death	1117
1731	1758	Love can do all but raise the dead	1758
431	389	Me come my dazzled face	0389
27	18	Morns like these we parted	0018
151	133	Mute thy coronation	0133
484	469	My garden like the beach	0469
95	74	My nosegays are for captives	0074
639	704	My portion is defeat today	0704
515	653	No crowd that has occurred	0653
1539	1575	Now I lay thee down to sleep	1575
653	462	Of being is a bird	0462
146	84	On such a night or such a night	0084
940	924	On that dear frame the years had worn	0924

Johnson #	Franklin #	Emily Dickinson title/first line	relates to *hE!* #
N/A	1478	One note from one bird	1478
14	5	One sister have I in the house	0005
251	271	Over the fence	0271
379	664	Rehearsal to ourselves	0664
.1182	1234	Remembrance has a rear and front	1234
1033	988	Said death to passion	0988
1385	1494	Secrets is a daily word	1494
507	351	She sights a bird she chuckles	0351
1251	1300	Silence is all we dread	1300
688	193	Speech is a prank of parliament	0193
1436	1460	Than heaven more remote	1460
1612	1646	The auctioneer of parting	1646
111	113	The bee is not afraid of me	0113
1274	1218	The bone that has no marrow	1218
284	255	The drop that wrestles in the sea	0255
1686	1724	The event was directly behind him	1724
18*	21	The gentian weaves her fringes	0021
707	779	The grace myself might not obtain	0779
1248	1172	The incidents of love	1172
1592	1613	The lassitudes of contemplation	1613
1689	1731	The look of thee what is it like	1731
429	387	The moon is distant from the sea	0387
274	331	The only ghost I ever saw	0331
1226	1220	The popular heart is a cannon first	1220
539	659	The province of the saved	0659
232	246	The sun just touched the morning	0246
152	182	The sun kept stooping stooping low	0182
1693	1709	The sun retired to a cloud	1709
1079	1109	The sun went down no man looked on	1109
493	280	The world stands solemner to me	0280
1094	1054	Themself are all I have	1054
1263	1286	There is no frigate like a book	1286
785	505	They have a little odor that to me	0505
613	445	They shut me up in prose	0445
1752	1769	This docile one inter	1769
1264	1284	This is the place they hoped before	1284
501	373	This world is not conclusion	0373
538	658	Tis true they shut me in the cold	0658
105	160	To hang our head ostensibly	0160
767	492	To offer brave assistance	0492

*Johnson 18 = Franklin 21, 22, 23

Johnson #	Franklin #	Emily Dickinson title/first line	relates to *hE!* #
911	902	Too little way the house must lie	0902
1028	1040	Twas my one glory	1040
972	839	Unfulfilled to observation	0839
1313	1307	Warm in her hand these accents lie	1307
1428	1446	Water makes many beds	1446
230	244	We bee and I live by the quaffing	0244
1175	1247	We like a hairbreadth 'scape	1247
1176	1197	We never know how high we are	1197
320	282	We play at paste	0282
1572	1619	We wear our sober dresses when we die	1619
996	503	We'll pass without the parting	0503
247	266	What would I give to see his face	0266
222	49	When Katie walks this simple pair accompany her side	0049
500	370	Within my garden rides a bird	0370
634	604	You'll know her by her foot	0604

EVERETT DECKER has been writing
poetry since the age of twelve. He
resides in his ancestral home in
Western Massachusetts, where the
henhouse his grandfather built
now garages his nine motorcycles.

CPSIA information can be obtained at www.ICGtesting.com
Printed in the USA
BVOW040727191211

278629BV00001B/5/P